Games

Around the World

Clare Lewis

Raintree

Raintree is an imprint of Capstone Global Library Limited, a company incorporated in England and Wales having its registered office at 7 Pilgrim Street, London, EC4V 6LB – Registered company number: 6695582

www.raintreepublishers.co.uk
myorders@raintreepublishers.co.uk

Edited by Joanna Issa, Shelly Lyons, Diyan Leake and Helen Cox Cannons
Designed by Cynthia Akiyoshi
Original illustrations © Capstone Global Library Ltd 2014
Picture research by Elizabeth Alexander and Tracy Cummins
Production by Victoria Fitzgerald
Originated by Capstone Global Library Ltd
Printed and bound in China

ISBN 978 1 406 28198 9
18 17 16 15 14
10 9 8 7 6 5 4 3 2 1

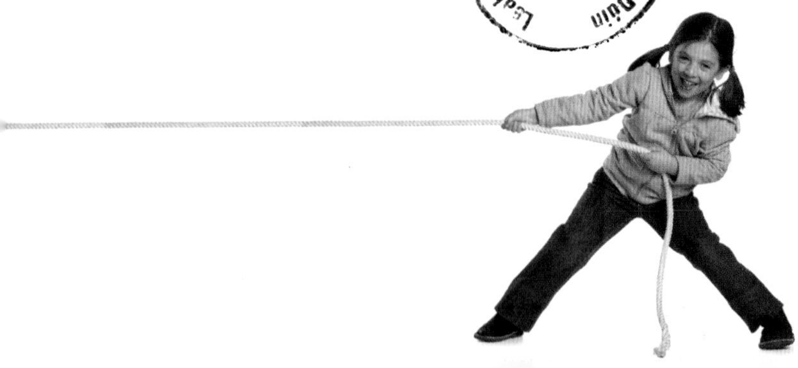

British Library Cataloguing in Publication Data
A full catalogue record for this book is available from the British Library.

Acknowledgements
We would like to thank the following for permission to reproduce photographs: Alamy pp. 4 (© Patrick Eden), 6 (© View Stock), 8 & 22c (both © AHOWDEN INTERNATIONAL), 12 & 22e (both © Peter Horree), 15 & 23 (both © Neil McAllister), 16 (© David Litschel); Getty Images pp. 5 & 22a (both Manfred Gottschalk), 10 (David Patrick Valera), 11 & 23 (both Jacek Chabraszewski), 13 & 22d (both Fuse), 17 (Simon Watson), 18 (Fabrice LEROUGE), 20 (JGI/Jamie Grill), 21 (Tim Hall); Shutterstock pp. 1 (© 2happy), 2 (© effe45), 3 (© pio3), 7 (© Kirk Peart Professional Imaging); Superstock pp. 9 (PhotoAlto), 14 (© Chevalier Virginie / Oredia Eurl), 19 & 22b (both Travel Library Limited). Design elements Shutterstock (© Tomislav Forgo, © Olga Popova, © Dan Kosmayer, © Africa Studio, © RTimages, © STILLFX).

Cover photograph of Masai tribe member in Kenya playing football reproduced with permission of SuperStock (Ton Koene / age fotostock). Back cover photograph reproduced with permission of Superstock (© Chevalier Virginie / Oredia Eurl).

Contents

Games everywhere

All around the world, children play games.

Grown-ups play games, too.

People play games for fun.

Sometimes people watch other people playing games.

Games with friends

People play games with their friends.

Friends can play games with pens and paper.

Games alone

People play games alone.

People play games on screens.

Different types of games

People play ball games.

People play football.

People play games with cards.

People play board games.

People play skipping games.

People play clapping games.

People play games with sticks.

People play games with stones.

People play make-believe games.

What games do you like to play?

Map of games around the world

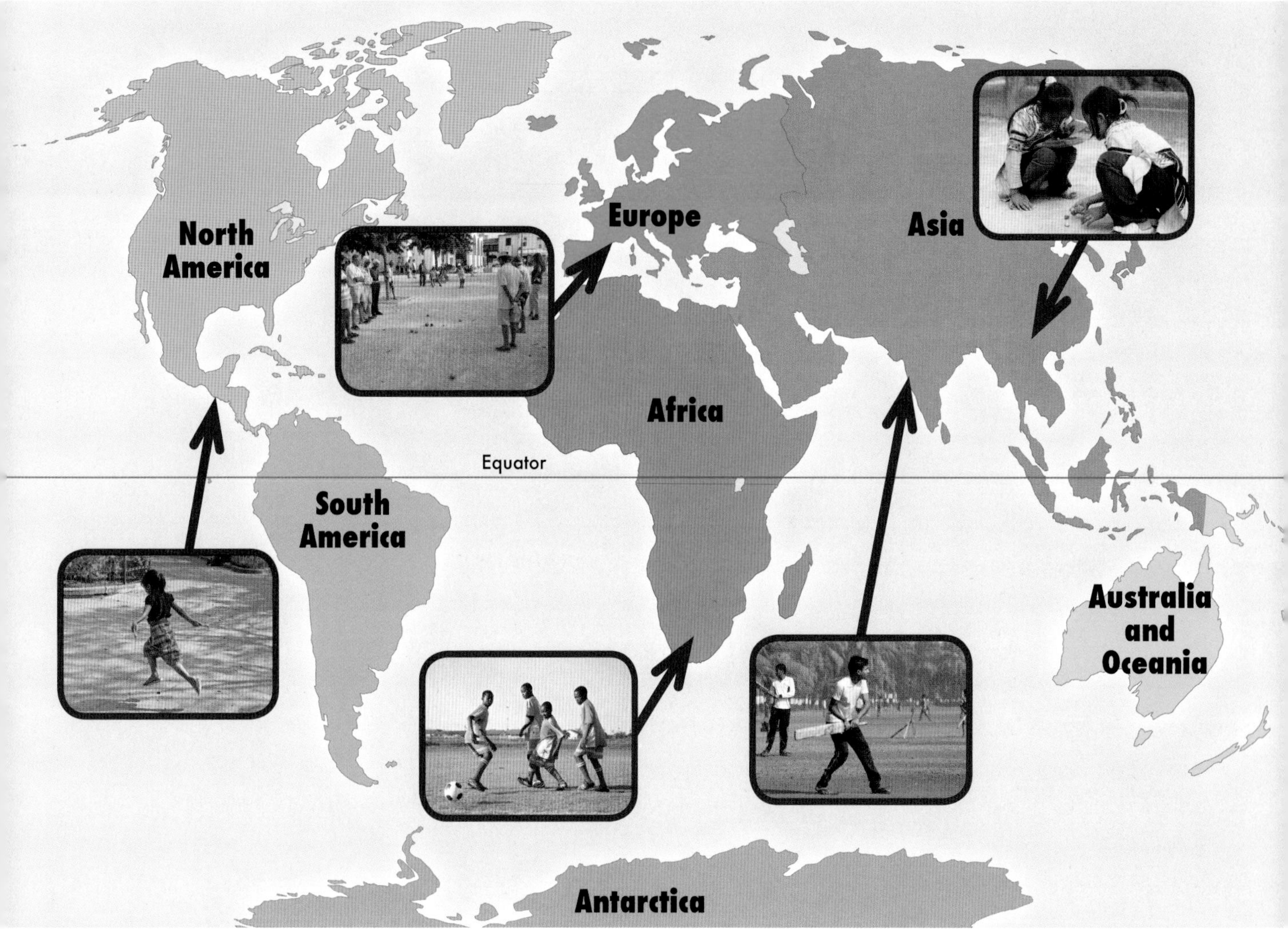

Picture glossary

board game game that has pieces that are moved along a board

screen the part of a computer or tablet that you look at to see the pictures or writing

Index

Notes for parents and teachers

Before reading

Read the title of the book and then write the word 'games' on the board. Ask children to name some games they know about, recording their answers as a list. Turn to page 24 of the book and explain that the index is a tool that helps readers find specific information in a book. Read the index entries and notice if there are any items that are similar to the list on the board. Demonstrate how to use the index to find the page where that type of game is mentioned.

After reading

- Review the list made before reading the book. Ask children if they learned about any other types of game from reading the book. Add them to the list.
- Turn to the map on page 22 and identify the seven continents with children. Discuss how this book is about games that are played all over the world, and demonstrate how this map is a tool that identifies where some of the photos were taken.
- Discuss that games often have rules that players must follow. Have children identify a familiar game (such as a game played at break time) and make a list of rules that they follow when they play the game. Depending on the age and ability of the children, you might have them work in pairs, or it could be a whole class activity.

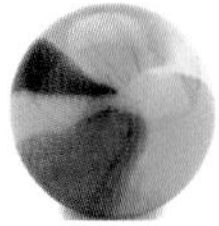